MAPLE SUGAR TIME

3417

The true story of two boys who visited their grandfather's farm in Marshfield, Vermont, during the sugar season. They rode on the sap sled, helped scatter the buckets, boiled the sap, drew off the syrup (learning what a lot of sap it takes to make a gallon of syrup) and finally they had a real sugaring-off party with all the sugar on snow they could eat.

The photographs are supplemented by drawings which are not only authentic but completely in the atmosphere of a Vermont sugar place.

This flavorful, entertaining, and simply written book—recommended by the American Library Association, May Lamberton Becker, Lewis Gannett, the Horn Book, and others—has become a classic for young people from six to ten years of age.

MAPLE SUGAR TIME

By Royce S. Pitkin

Headmaster, New London School, New London, New Hampshire

Formerly Supervising Principal

Wallingford, Vermont

Illustrated with Drawings

BY CLIFFORD A. BAYARD

and with Photographs

STEPHEN DAYE PRESS

New York

The Murray Printing Company, Cambridge, Mass., U.S.A.

DEDICATED TO THE TWO BOYS
WHO MADE THIS A TRUE STORY

EDITOR'S NOTE

Those teachers who wish to develop an interested and active group of individuals in their reading classes may welcome these suggestions.

If you live in a region where sugaring is carried on, make an effort to take your children to the sugar house. If yours is not a sugaring region, there may be children whose parents or neighbors have lived in sugaring states; first-hand information might be secured from this source. But whatever the environment in which this book is used, it is the type of informational reader that offers a splendid opportunity to introduce the study of geography. This study may include not only location of states and cities mentioned, but may extend to climate and differences in seasons.

Maple Sugar Time is illustrated with actual photographs of operations on a typical Vermont sugar place, supplemented by drawings also made on the scene of operations. Much profitable discussion can center around these illustrations, for children like *real* things.

While this book derives from the maple groves of Vermont, it should be kept in mind that sugaring is carried on in a number of other northern states. The leading states, in the order of their production totals of 1932, are Vermont,

New York, Pennsylvania, New Hampshire, Massachusetts, Michigan, Ohio, Wisconsin, and Maine. There are similarities and differences in operations in these various regions, dependent on climate, soil, and kinds of maple trees; but in all of them, as in Vermont, there is a "maple sugar time."

ACTIVITIES

Some classes will find it worth while to make a sugar place, with the sugar house and as much of the equipment as the supply of materials at hand permits. It may be that some members of the class will wish to make drawings of the sugar season's activities. This should be encouraged.

› Every class should experience the making of maple sugar. If there are maple trees in your community, by all means let the pupils bring in enough maple sap to make a little syrup. A valuable lesson in science can be taught by doing that. If you have no maple trees, you can secure some maple syrup from the grocery stores. By mixing a little of this syrup with water, a fair imitation of maple sap can be had. Of course real maple sap looks like water and is slightly sweet.

The children will want a sugaring-off party. If you are careful, a pint of good syrup will serve for quite a large class. This should be boiled in a dish that holds at least a quart. You should have a little butter or cream at hand to put on the sugar when it begins to rise in the dish, other wise, it is likely to boil over. If you have snow, use it for the sugar on snow. Simply pour a little on a dish of snow that has been packed down carefully. If the sugar is done, it will form a hard gum. You can use ice in place of snow with very good results. And, if you have neither ice nor snow, pour the hot sugar into glasses of cold water. Soft balls will form, as when candy is tested.

VOCABULARY

The vocabulary of this book has been carefully chosen so that it is well within the range of good first-grade readers. However, the content of the story is such that it will be appealing even to the fourth-grade child. This range, unusual in primary readers, adds greatly to the flexibility and utility of the book.

TESTS

The comprehension tests in the back of the book are easily accessible either for testing after each chapter or for general review. They are separated from the text to avoid destroying the integrity of the story.

John Hooper.

Contents

Chapter I

THE LETTER FROM GRANDMA

It was a warm day in March.

Big white snowflakes were falling.

Don and Bob were sorry, as they looked out of the window. They were sorry because spring couldn't come while the snow was still on the ground.

"Do you know what kind of snow this is?" asked their mother.

"Yes, it's a bad snow."

"Oh no. This is a real sugar snow."

"What do you mean by sugar snow?" asked the boys.

"Well, sugar snow is the kind of snow that comes when it is time for sugaring," their mother answered. "Maybe Grandpa is getting ready to make sugar today."

Then the two boys shouted, "Let's go up to Grandpa's tomorrow. There is no school all next week."

"Maybe we can. We will see what Daddy has to say about it when he comes home," said their mother.

"Here is Daddy, now," said Don.

"He has a letter, too. Who is the mail for, Daddy?" asked Bob before his father had time to speak.

"It is for two boys," he said as he gave it to them. The boys opened it as fast as they could and this is what they found.

Marshfield, Vermont.
March 15.

Dear Bob and Don:

It is almost time for sugaring. Grandpa is getting ready to wash the buckets now. We want you to come up and visit us when you have your vacation. We will have some sugar on snow.

George wants me to tell you that you may ride on the sap sled and drive the horses.

Tell your mother and daddy that we want them to come, too.

With love,

Grandma

The rest of this book tells what Don and Bob saw when they went to their grandfather's farm in Vermont.

Chapter II

THE SUGAR HOUSE

The first day they were there they went for a ride to the sugar house in the woods. The sugar house is the place where maple sugar is made. But they didn't ride on the train.

They didn't ride in a car. They didn't ride in a wagon. They didn't ride in an airplane. They had their ride on a sled.

The big sled was pulled by two horses. Their names were Dick and Prince. The hired man drove them. His name was George. The boys thought it was great fun to ride through the snow with almost no noise.

At the sugar house Grandpa and another hired man were building a fire. The fire was in a big stove which they called an arch. On the top of the arch was a big pan. ' The

The Sugaring Off Arch

pan was five feet long and two feet wide. It was a foot deep. It was called the sugaring-off pan.

The men put snow into the pan. Of course the snow changed into water. When the water was hot the men used it to wash the sap buckets. After each bucket was washed it was put in the pan of hot water for a minute. Then the buckets were put out in the sun to dry. After the buckets were dry they were ready to go on the big sled.

By the time all of the buckets were washed the sun was hiding behind the trees. So all of the men and boys jumped on the big sled.

"Get up, Dick. Go along, Prince," said George. And the horses started for the house.

"Who would like to drive?" asked George.

"I would," Bob and Don shouted together.

"Well, I guess we will have to take turns," said Grandpa. "Bob can drive half of the way and Don can drive the other half."

What fun it was to drive the big horses! The boys felt like big men as they said "Gee, Prince" and "Haw, Dick" to make the horses keep in the road.

Supper was ready by the time they came to the house. Bob and Don were ready for it. The work at the sugar place had made them hungry. But their grandmother had lots of good things to eat.

After supper Grandpa said to the boys "Did you ever hear how maple sugar was first made?"

"No. Won't you tell us how?" asked the boys.

"It was this way," said Grandpa. "Once upon a time an Indian mother was cooking some meat for her family. While it was boiling in the pot she was busy at other work. The first thing she knew the water was almost gone from the pot and the meat began to burn. So she ran toward the spring for more water. On her way she saw a dish by a maple tree. There was some kind of water in it for some one had cut the tree a little and the sap had run into the dish.

"The Indian mother ran back with the sap and put it into her meat and let it boil. But when she looked at it later it was thick and brown. She was afraid it would not be good and that was all she had for her hungry family to eat for dinner.

"The father and the children came to eat. They took out pieces of the meat. It was so sticky that the father said, 'This must be a new kind of meat.' The mother said nothing, she was so afraid.

"How surprised she was when the father ate some and shouted, 'My, this is good! How did you make it?' And she said, 'I boiled it in the sap of the maple tree.'

"And that is the way maple sugar was first made."

Their day in the sugar woods began to make the boys quite sleepy. By the time Grandpa finished his story, they could just keep their eyes open. When they climbed the stairs to their beds they were almost asleep. They could keep their eyes open just long enough to hear Grandpa say, "Boys, if tomorrow is a good day we will scatter the buckets and start tapping the trees."

They couldn't even keep their eyes and ears open to find out what it means to tap a tree.

Chapter III
BOYS WITH BUCKETS

While the boys were asleep, the night grew cold. In the morning the snow that had been soft and wet the day before was hard and cold as ice. The bright sun made it shine with many little lights.

At the breakfast table, Grandpa told the boys that the snow was so cold and hard that it made a good crust.

"The crust is strong enough to hold you up. It will be a good day to scatter the buckets."

"But why do you want to scatter them?" asked Bob.

"We have to put one by each tree. When we tap we can hang them on the trees," answered Grandpa.

"Can we help?" asked the boys as they ate their breakfast in a hurry.

After breakfast, George hitched the horses to the big sled. The men

and boys climbed on for their ride to
the sugar house.

At the sugar house a lot of buckets
were put on the sled.

"It looks to me as though we would

have to break a road," said George.

"But what do you want to break a road for?" asked the boys. "Don't you want to use it?"

"It's funny," said Grandpa, "but when you break a road, you make one."

"You are joking with us now," laughed Don. "How can you make a road when you break it?"

"It is this way," said Grandpa. "When we make a road in the woods where there is a lot of snow, we have to break the crust down. As we break the crust we make a road."

Then George began to drive the

horses into the woods. The snow was deep and the boys could not see a thing that looked like a road. Dick and Prince slowly made their way through the crust. But they had to stop for a rest very often. The load was heavy and the snow made walking very hard for them.

Every time the horses stopped to rest, George would pull a bucket out and throw it on the snow near a tree. Sometimes he would take some buckets under his arm and carry them to the trees far from the road.

The boys also carried buckets to the trees. At first they made some

mistakes. What do you suppose the mistakes were?

George didn't leave buckets for every tree but the boys had not seen that. Both boys ran about on the crust and put buckets near every tree that looked big enough. When they left four buckets near some trees with green tops George saw them. He began to laugh and laugh.

"What is the trouble?" asked the boys.

"I didn't think to tell you that we tap only maple trees. Those trees with the green tops are evergreen trees. We can't make sugar from their sap. Maple trees have no leaves at this time of year. Their bark is rough and gray. See, like this."

So the boys learned how to tell

maple trees from the many others in the woods.

As the men and boys worked, the day grew warm. By noon the crust was soft and the boys could not walk on it as they had in the morning.

"I think sap will run today," said Grandpa, "I think we should start tapping right after dinner."

Chapter IV

TAPPING THE TREES

After dinner Grandpa and Herbert, the other hired man, took some spouts like those in the picture. They put the spouts in a little pail so they could carry them. Then they each took a hammer and a bit and brace and went out to tap the trees.

The boys watched closely, for they did not want to miss a thing. They

saw Grandpa walk through the deep
snow till he came to a maple tree.
Then he looked around for a good
place to begin tapping.

When he found a smooth place he made a hole with his bit right through the bark into the wood. After he pulled his bit out of the hole he was very careful to blow out all of the tiny pieces of wood.

Then he took one of the little spouts from his pail and put it into the hole. He used his hammer to drive it in tight.

Each little spout had a hook on it. So Grandpa took one of the buckets that the boys had put by the tree and let it hang on the hook. He could do this because there was a little hole in the bucket near the top.

The spout hook went into this hole.

When the bucket was on the hook, both boys watched to see what happened. Pretty soon a little drop of water came out of the spout. It stopped for a moment at the end of the spout.

Then it fell to the bottom of the iron bucket and made a soft little bang. But right behind it came another little drop. And then another. And another! And still another!

The drops came so fast that they made a little orchestra.

Drop! Drop! Drop! Drop!

These little drops of water were sap from the maple tree.

After each bucket was put on its hook, the men would put a cover over it. This cover kept the snow and rain and dirt from falling into the sap.

After many of the trees were tapped, the boys could hear the tinkle of the drops in the buckets all around them. It made a sound like music.

Chapter V

GATHERING THE SAP

In a few days, after all of the trees had been tapped and all of the buckets had been scattered, Grandpa said to Bob and Don, "How would you like to gather sap today?"

"Fine!" they shouted.

"Well, I think we will find a lot of it. We will have to start boiling soon," said Grandpa.

The boys had another ride on the big sled with George. When they got to the sugar house, George and Herbert put a big iron tank on the

sap sled. They each took two big
pails that they called "gathering
pails."

Then the horses began to pull the sled again and the boys had to hang on to the big tank which was almost as big as the sled.

Pretty soon the men took their pails and walked through the deep snow to the trees with the buckets. They poured the sap from the buckets into their big pails. Then they carried the pails back to the sled and poured the sap into the tank.

If you look at the picture of Herbert on page 38, you can see how deep the snow was that day. He has a gathering pail in one hand.

As the horses pulled the sled

along, the boys could hear the sap banging against the sides of the tank. But it couldn't get out.

'After gathering the sap from all of the trees on that road, George let the boys drive the horses to the hill just above the sugar house. The horses did not go very fast because the tank was full of sap and it was very heavy.

"Just think," said Bob. "All of that sap came out of the trees in tiny drops. How could there be so much in the tank now?"

"I know. It's just like the rain drops filling up a lake," said Don.

"Only these drops are sweet," Bob replied.

"What makes them sweet, Daddy?" asked Don.

"They are sweet because the leaves on the trees made some sugar last summer," answered their father.

"What did they make the sugar out of? Did Grandpa put some sugar on the ground?" asked Don.

"No. The green part of the leaves made the sugar out of water that came up from the roots of the trees. We don't know just how the leaves do it, but they do."

"But where does the sugar stay all winter?" asked Bob.

"It stays in the stems and the roots. Then when spring comes and we have cold nights and warm days, the sap begins to go up and down the tree. It is sugaring-time then. If it is warm every night and day, the

Things the · Maple Tree · uses in · storing up .. sugar ..

sap won't run and we can't get any in the buckets," said Daddy. "That is why they don't make maple sugar in most states."

"Oh, see the sap run! It's just like a river," said Don, as George let

41

the sap out of the tank through a big pipe on the end.

The sap ran into a long wood pipe and on down the hill into a still bigger tank. This tank was about as large as the tanks on the gasoline trucks. It was called the storage tank because the sap was kept there until it was used in the sugar house.

Chapter VI

MAKING THE SYRUP

After the sap had run out of the gathering tank, the boys went for a ride with the men to get another load.

When they came back to the sugar house what do you think they saw?

They saw a big gray cloud coming out of the top of the sugar house. But it was not coming out of the tall chimney. As they watched it, more and more came out.

"The sugar house is burning up!" shouted the boys. "What shall we

do? Hurry, Daddy, and put out the fire."

"I don't think the sugar house is burning," said their father. "Let's go down and see what is going on."

So down to the sugar house they went.

As they stepped in the door they saw their grandfather throwing big

The Evaporator

pieces of wood into a hot fire in the big arch. This arch was much longer than the sugaring-off arch. This one was longer than some automobiles. On top of it was a big pan with many little rooms in it. This pan is called an evaporator. Clouds of steam were coming off from it. The boys had thought they were clouds of smoke.

"What are you doing, Grandpa?" asked Bob.

"I am boiling," said Grandpa.

"Gee, what are you going to wash with all of that water?" asked Don.

"We don't wash with that. That is the sap that you helped gather this morning. We are now making it into syrup," said Grandpa.

"The water in the sap is boiling out and leaving the sugar," their father told the boys. "When enough of the water is boiled out we will have some syrup. It takes about forty gallons of sap to make one gallon of syrup."

"But why doesn't the sugar boil out, too?" asked Don.

"Because sugar can't turn into steam the way water does. When it gets too hot it burns."

"How does the sap get into this pan?" asked Bob.

"See the pipe that is on top of the evaporator?" asked Grandpa. "That goes to the big tank and the sap runs down through it into the evaporator. By the time it gets to this last corner it is sweeter and more

sticky than it was when it started. You watch me now."

Then both boys watched their grandfather. He took a bucket and went over to the corner of the evaporator where the sap had boiled till it was very sweet. Then he turned a little pipe that was on the side of the pan. And the sweet golden sap ran into the bucket until it was half full.

"There is the first syrup we have made this year," said Grandpa. "Who would like to eat some of it?"

"I would," shouted Bob.

"So would I," said Don.

"And so would I," said their father.

"Wait a minute till I strain it and you can have all you want," said Grandpa.

Then he went to a big tin can that stood on end. The top end had a heavy cloth over it. Grandpa poured the bucket of hot syrup into the heavy cloth. This strained out all the tiny pieces of dirt.

As soon as the syrup was strained, the boys had some dishes filled. And how they did eat!

"Gee, isn't this good," shouted Bob.

"Daddy, why don't you get a sugar place so we can have maple syrup every day?" asked Don.

Chapter VII

THE SYRUP TRAVELS

"Grandpa, how do you eat all of your syrup?" asked Bob.

"Well, we don't eat very much of it, only when the grandchildren are here. We sell most of it," said Grandpa.

"Where do you sell it?" asked the boys.

"Oh, we sell it in many places. We send some to Boston, some to New York, some to Chicago. Yesterday we had a letter from a man in California who wants to buy some. People in

California buy the sugar we make in Vermont and people in Vermont buy the grapes and oranges that grow out there," Grandpa said.

"How do you get it to all of those places?" asked Don.

"First of all we put it in these tin cans." And Grandpa showed them some cans that would hold a gallon of maple syrup.

He then showed the boys how the cans were filled with the new syrup. He held a can under the pipe at the bottom of the big can and the syrup ran into it.

"Now we have to put the syrup's

name on the can." And Grandpa put some paste on a piece of paper that said on it PURE MAPLE SYRUP. He pasted the paper on the can that he had just filled.

"People will know that it is real maple syrup," said Grandpa.

"When we get down to the house we will make a box to put the can in. Then we will write the name of the man it is for on the top of the box. We will put some stamps on it and leave it by the mail box. When the mailman comes he will take it to the post office. From the post office it will go to the railroad station. Then the train will take it to the right city. It takes many workers to get Grandpa's sugar to the people who buy it."

"Bob and I are going to live on a farm when we are big. Aren't we Bob?" said Don.

"Yes, we are. On a farm you can have lots of sugar and milk and almost everything," said his brother.

Chapter VIII

SUGAR ON SNOW

One morning, when vacation and the snow were both almost gone, Grandma said, "Who would like to go to a sugaring-off today?"

The boys were not quite sure what a sugaring-off was but they both shouted, "I would."

"All right. Grandpa says we can have one this afternoon," Grandma said. "We will hurry and tell all the neighbors. And Uncle John and his family are coming today. We will have many people there."

That afternoon it was very warm as the boys climbed the hill to the sugar house with their grandfather. They saw him pour four buckets of syrup into the sugaring-off pan. Then he built a hot fire in the arch with short pieces of dry wood from the shed by the sugar house door.

Soon the people began to come. Boys and girls came. Old men and women came. Lots of people came. Most of them brought little dishes or tin cups to put some sugar in.

"Who wants a paddle?" asked the boys' father.

"We do," said the boys.

But they didn't know what kind of a paddle. And they didn't know what the paddle was for.

Their father took an axe and cut a piece of wood from a clean maple stick. Then with his knife he made a paddle that was about as long as a table knife. He gave this to one boy. Then he made another for the other boy and one for himself.

"Now let's see what the sugar is doing," he said.

They went into the sugar house. There they saw the syrup boiling in the pan. As it boiled, thousands of little bubbles came to the top of

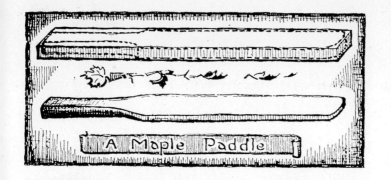

A Maple Paddle

it. They rose higher and higher in the pan.

"Oh Grandpa," shouted Don, "your syrup is growing taller. It is going to fall out of the pan."

"We must fix that," said Grandpa.

And he took a little cream out of a cup and scattered it over the bubbling sugar. The bubbles began to break and fall and soon the sugar was no longer near the top of the pan. But a little later it rose again and more cream was put on it to keep it from boiling over the side of the pan.

"If some one will get a bucket of snow, we will have some sugar on snow," said Grandpa.

So some of the men got buckets of snow. Grandpa took a dipper and poured the hot sugar on the snow. The cold snow made it sticky. The boys took their paddles and pulled up big lumps of the sugar. It was like gum. They put the lumps in their mouths. The lumps were so

sticky that they could hardly talk.

But they ate and ate. It was so good!

After all the people had had all the sugar on snow they wanted, they poured a little sugar in their dishes. They stirred the soft sticky sugar with their wooden paddles until it was quite stiff and almost white. This made very good candy.

When the sugar in the sugaring-off pan had boiled for a while Grandpa put a thermometer in it.

"What do you put that thermometer in the sugar for?" asked Bob.

"That tells how hot the sugar is. The longer it boils, the hotter it gets," said Grandpa. "When it gets hot enough it will be done."

After he had read the thermometer many times, Grandpa shouted, "It's done! Who will help me?"

Then four men took the pan of

sugar off the fire. They put it on a low table to let it cool a little.

As the sugar grew colder, Grandpa stirred it with a big wooden paddle. This made the sugar thick and heavy. Pretty soon he poured it into small pails. The next morning the sugar was hard. After he had put papers on them which said PURE MAPLE SUGAR, they were ready to sell. Perhaps you have seen pails like them in stores.

It was soon time for Bob and Don and their father to go back home. They took with them a large can of maple syrup to eat on pancakes.

They also took a pail of the maple sugar to eat on bread.

"It will taste even better than ever, since we helped make it," said the boys.

[THE END]

THIS PART OF THE BOOK
WILL HELP YOU
REMEMBER THE STORY

TESTS

Chapter I

After each sentence there are four words. On a piece of paper write the word that makes the sentence correct.

1. The snow made Don and Bob........
   sick, sorry, tall, short.

2. Mother said, "This is a real.........
   snow."
   sugar, some, white, bad.

3. Daddy had a.........
   letter, butter, sugar, lamb.

4. This story tells about a.........
   school, fox, farm, fat.

5. The letter was for the.........
   father, mother, boys, box.

6. The letter was from.........
   Grandpa, Grandma, George,
   grass.

7. The day was.........
   cold, clean, warm, water.

8. The letter said "It is almost
   time for.........
   playing, snowing, sugaring,
   school.

9. The boys wanted to go to.........
   Grandpa's, sing, school, Green.

10. The farm was in.........
    Very, Vermont, warm, white.

Chapter II

From the phrases at the bottom of the next page, pick the right one for each sentence. On a piece of paper write the numbers 1 to 10. After each number write the letter that tells the right phrase.

1. The boys had a ride.........

2. There was a fire.........

3. The sun was hiding.........

4. George said to the horses "........."

5. The sugar house is.........

6. Grandma had lots of good.........

7. The men put snow.........

8. The horses' names were.........

9. Maple sugar was first
   made by.........

10. The Indian mother put sap.........

Phrases

a. in the woods

b. on a sled

c. get up, Dick

d. in the arch

e. behind the trees

f. things to eat

g in the meat

h. Dick and Prince

i. the Indian mother

j. into the pan

Chapter III

On a piece of paper write the numbers from 1 to 5. After each number write the letter that tells which phrase makes the best answer for that sentence.

1. The sun made the snow shine
    a. with sugar
    b. with little lights
    c. with moon light

2. George hitched the horses
    a. to the big sled
    b. to the big stars
    c. to the trees

3. The men and boys had a ride
   a. in the airplane
   b. in the wagon
   c. to the sugar house

4. When the boys put buckets by the trees with the green tops
   a. they were right
   b. they made sugar
   c. they made a mistake

5. The bark of maple trees is
   a. white and smooth
   b. rough and gray
   c. soft and gray

Chapter IV

Answer each question with "Yes" or "No"

1. Did Grandpa put some spouts in a little pail?

2. Did the men take a hammer?

3. Did Grandpa ride to the tree?

4. Did Grandpa put a spout in the hole in the tree?

5. Did Grandpa use his bit to drive the spout?

6. Was there a hook on
   each spout?

7. Did the bucket hang
   on the spout?

8. Did the sap make a
   lot of noise?

9. Was the bucket made of wood?

10. Does the cover keep out rain?

Chapter V

Match each phrase at the bottom of the next page with the right sentence.

1. George and Herbert put......... on the sap sled.

2. The men poured sap from the buckets into.........

3. George let the boys.........

4. When the tank was full of sap.........

5. The sap came out of the trees.........

6. The sap was sweet
   because the.........

7. The sap ran from the tank.........

8. Don said "See the sap run!
   It's just........."

Words and Phrases

a. drive the horses

b. it was very heavy

c. a big iron tank

d. in tiny drops

e. the gathering pails

f. leaves made sugar

g. like a river

h. into a long wood pipe

Chapter VI

After each sentence there are three phrases. On a piece of paper write the letter that tells which phrase makes the sentence correct.

1. A big gray cloud came
    a. out of the ground
    b. out of the chimney
    c. out of the top of the sugar house

2. The clouds of steam came from
    a. Grandpa's pipe
    b. the boiling sap
    c. the horses

3. When water boils out of the sap
   a. it leaves sugar
   b. it is cold
   c. it leaves snow

4. Don and Bob ate
   a. sugar on snow
   b. some sap
   c. some new syrup

5. Don wanted Daddy to get
   a. an automobile
   b. a sugar place
   c. a sap bucket

Chapter VII

After each sentence there are two phrases. On a piece of paper write the letter that tells which phrase makes the sentence correct.

1. Grandpa sells his syrup
   - a. in many places
   - b. in the woods

2. Grandpa had a letter from a man in
   - a. Vermont
   - b. California

3. The mailman takes the boxes to
   a. the post office
   b. the right city

4. Bob said "On a farm you can have lots of
   a. fresh air"
   b. sugar and milk."

Chapter VIII

Write the numbers from 1 to 9 on a sheet of paper. Pick a word from the list at the bottom of the next page and write it after the number of the question which it answers. Do this for all of the words.

1. Who said "Who would like to go to a sugaring-off today?"

2. What did Grandpa put into the sugaring-off pan?

3. What did the boys' father make for them?

4. What did Grandpa put in the sugar so it would not boil over?

5. What did the men put in the buckets?

6. What did the people make with the sugar in their dishes?

7. What did Grandpa pour on the snow?

8. Who took the pan of sugar off the fire?

9. What tells how hot the sugar is?

Words

candy	syrup	four men
Grandma	a paddle	cream
snow	thermometer	sugar